A LITTLE LAZARUS

A Little Lazarus

poems by Mendy Knott

Half Acre Press
Fayetteville
2010

Copyright © 2010 by Mendy Knott
All rights reserved
Manufactured in the United States of America

No part of this book may be reproduced or utilized in any form or by any means, electronic or mechanical, including photocopying and recording, or by any information storage and retrieval system, without permission in writing from the publisher.

ISBN-13: 978-0-9829455-1-3

Designed by Liz Lester

HALF
ACRE
PRESS

halfacrepress.com

To Leigh
—and to my friend Jane

CONTENTS

Acknowledgments *ix*

Body

Mt. Moriah or Why God Won't Talk to Women 3
Where I'm From 8
Ode to a Day 10
Baptism 13
Reflecting Paul 15
Education 17
A Dozen Ways of Looking at Thirteen 20
Born Again 23
The Giving Tree 25
Where is the Prince of Peace? 29
Before You Jump 33
Revival 36

Blood

The Straight Dope 43
How Love Changes the World 46
Ode to the Dark 49
Death in the Holler 50
Dress Blues 55
Opera Light 56
Seeds 58
Burst of Light: A Tribute to Audre Lorde 59
Touch Wood 63
There is no moral to the story 65

Subtraction   68
Iraq/Afghanistan War Heroes Dot Com   71
Memento   74
Body Electric   75
The Gold Pocket Watch   77

Communion

A Little Lazarus   81
For Walt Whitman   83
Rules of the Road   85
Photo Op   86
Peacework   87
Sunrise Service   90
Ode to Morning   92
Peace in Small Packages   94
Friday Nights in Yancey County   96
A Fisherman's Grace   97
The Moon's Distant Call   99
Leaving   100

ACKNOWLEDGMENTS

My mom's family told stories in the shade of an Arkansas white oak while they shelled peas or hand-cranked ice cream. Raised in the Bible Belt by a minister father, my first iambic pentameter was biblical. Adam and Eve, Abraham and Sarah, Jesus and Lazarus peopled my daily life and imagination. I thank my parents for this gift of story that has accompanied me on roads far from those of my childhood—and back again. After eighteen years of writing, reading and performing poetry, I still love the oral tradition and heartily believe that poetry belongs to the people, to everyone.

I also want to thank my chosen family of friends, who have kept my home fires burning even when I seemed lost and far away from home. Their inspiration and encouragement have fed me throughout the years. I thank Liz Lester for her faith in me and for wanting Half Acre Press to publish my words. I'm honored to have Path Hennon's fine art on my cover. And as always, I could not have accomplished this phase of my work without Leigh Wilkerson standing beside me as part of my daily life.

Finally, to the poets you see on the back page of this book who first heard my words and said, "Girl, you got a gift," and to every single one of you who read these poems and are inspired to write your own, I offer you my undying gratitude.

Thank you to the publications in which the following poems first appeared:

Asheville Poetry Review and *Best of Asheville Poetry Review*: Revival

Passages Through Poetry (Caversham Press, South Africa): Mt. Moriah or Why God Won't Talk to Women, A Little Lazarus

Peacework: Poems in Wartime (CD): Peace is Personal, Peace in Small Packages

Raising Voices: A Café-of-Our-Own Anthology: The Straight Dope, Leaving

Western North Carolina Woman: Peacework

The Witness (thewitness.org): Where is the Prince of Peace?

Womonwrites Anthology 1998: Education, How Love Changes the World

Body

Mt. Moriah or Why God Won't Talk to Women

for Sarah Jewel Cross

To the woman He said, "I will greatly multiply your pain in childbearing; in sorrow thou shalt bring forth children."

—GENESIS 3.16

In "Bible Stories for Children" Mt. Moriah looked like this:
Lush green hills, a little like the Ozarks
a few boulders scattered for effect
an altar built of sticks and stones
blue sky, dawn light, and Abraham sprawled across poor Isaac
rope-wound hands and feet
a look of total disbelief staring up
at his old man, this old man
who doted on him day and night
then led him lamblike to be slaughtered.
Abraham's face, little more than sculpted stone
itself, dead serious.
God had talked to him, had said,
"Sacrifice the boy.
Sacrifice your child.
Sacrifice the seed of Israel.
Sacrifice your only son,
your son."
And so he would.
Knife raised high above his head
blade glinting in the sun's first rays
an angel gorgeous as a gay boy right behind him
reaching to prevent the descent
of dagger into breastbone.
Nearby in the bushes

a ram caught by the horns—
scapegoat to be sliced and diced and roasted for God's pleasure.

When I asked my reverend father what he would have done
he would not lie.
Was it then I began to doubt God's sincerity
His love for me?
Or later when I thought of Sarah all alone
waiting for her menfolk to come home?
What would Abraham have said?
"God told me to. I did."
Bet that would have gone over big.

God won't talk to women.
Ever notice that?
He knows mothers, daughters, sisters
they be talking back,
"Say WHAT? You want me to do WHAT?
After all I been through with this boy—
birthing him at ninety (or nineteen)
feeding him my tit
dressing him, undressing him
bathing his body
combing his hair
patching his wounds
tasting his tears.
Now You say You want him BACK?
Give me one good reason, God . . .
no, faith is not enough.
Jump back, Jehovah!
You've lost your mind
'cause you ain't taking mine."

Close the book.
Turn the page;
story from a different age—
Mt. Moriah of my childhood.

Walk with the woman I've become
down a two-lane blacktop in Deep Country, Arkansas
not far from Texas, close by Louisiana;
buttercups and daffodils bowing down in fields
where the heat hangs heavy as a stage curtain.
Turn left into a gravel lot where underneath a spreading oak
lean planks and broken benches and every Wednesday's
dinner-on-the-grounds and a good old-fashioned gospel sing.
Follow the limbs of that ancient oak until you see
green fingers scratch their leaves against the steeple
of an old white clapboard church, one room
no frills, no scroll, no stained glass windows,
no denomination to distinguish it from all the others
you've seen scattered along the highway.
Come on around back. There above the fence
in wrought iron letters bent and twisted
stained with rust, read "Mt. Moriah" above the gate.
Go ahead, open it, it's never locked.
Weave your way through countless graves and artificial flowers.
Beside a youngish elm near the fence that keeps the field at bay
she lies between her husband and her son.
Another Sarah, surrounded by her sacrifices
sole matriarch of the Camden Crosses,
ten which she bore proudly into the land of the living.
Two died young, two sons
they're buried here somewhere,
snatched without a word from God

without a single explanation, no discussion
not one breathless, whispered why.

Sarah bore eight more into a world at war
with little enough to eat, she fed them
clothed them, cured them from the measles.
She thought she was safe, having given it all
and her children grown and ready for work and the world
and the next war.
She was relieved, believing her sacrifices were complete
for she was old, well past her child-bearing years
when they came for her rebel son.
City cops bound his hands, beat his head,
locked him in an icy cell. No call from God
or from Camden's finest came
when that noxious halo slid
down past the damp brown curls
across the violet eyes. Hushed,
the knotting of the boxer's biceps
his final, choking cry.

God won't talk to women.
He sends messengers that say, "Hey, guess what?
Good news! You'll have a boy today."
What he doesn't say is how they'll die
at the hands of other men, in uniform or out.
There's a thousand causes, all good reasons
to cut a youngster down.
Any woman worth her salt will tell you, "Life
will kill you quick enough. No matter how strong,
No matter how tough.
There's no duty to go early.
Why drive back into darkness what we have brought to light?"
But God won't talk to women.

It broke her, Lanny's death;
bowed her down towards the ground
where she couldn't look up any longer into God's inscrutable face.
We laid Sarah beside her son, wrapped closely
in a blanket of Arkansas dust, red as the dying day.
As friends and family bowed to pray
I turned my face away in silent sacrilege
and returned her to the Mother.

Now is it any wonder that women have grown tired
of being constantly ignored?
Wanting to restore a feminine face to God,
they bestow her with breasts to feed her children
arms that embrace, hands that heal
and will not wield the knife.
Beneath a full moon,
in a circle,
around a morning coffee table—
when God's a woman She will talk
and God knows we need Someone
we can talk to.

Where I'm From

I am from Dick and Madelyn
Jethro and Jewel
Lillian and John (Jake to his buddies).
I am from deep beneath the tarnished buckle
of the Bible Belt.
Southern states have left traces
all over me like lint:
sweet dark molasses of Big Muddy in my accent
orange dusting of Texas hill country across my cheeks
the wild of a barefoot, small-town Louisiana child.
I'm from a long line of preacher men,
mostly Presbyterian, some Methodist,
all absolutely fundamental to:
my love of language
my tendency to tell a story
the long, lost lonely nights of young lesbians and liars.
I'm from my Mamaw's front porch swattin' flies,
Camden street lamps jarring junebugs,
farm ponds catching bream, bass, catfish, carp.
I am from every night a home-cooked meal,
hand-cranked ice cream in the summer
roastbeefriceandgravy on most Sundays.
As I was made once from my Momma's garden,
I'm now grown up in Leigh's green beans and red tomatoes.
I own the drunk I'm from, the addict born to bear
the brokenness of a woman soldier and big-city cop.
I am living proof there's a kind of universal grace:

born once, then
born again in AA
born again in creativity
born again in true love
born again each time I open up to hope.
I am from, as much as all of these,
black ink and blank white paper
the will to write, to change, to be.

Ode to a Day

Day, you awakened me with whispers
early, like a lover who has lain awake for hours
waiting, excited and impatient
for what you thought was long enough
then with a breeze that kissed my eyes awake
began sweet murmurings:
"Hey girl, get up.
Looky here what I have for you.
It's not December 25th, but it might as well be Christmas.
It's not your birthday, but I have presents.
Roll on over into me and let me be your greatest gift."

Then Day, you dripped butterscotch
all down my windowsill; it pooled
yellow on the floor where I was sure to step in it.
A broken blue horizon like a jack-o'-lantern's teeth
grinned in at me while I let you take me unobjecting
let you get inside me deep
let you make me come with you
wherever you would lead.
"Day," I said, "Take it away . . ."
And you did.

You, Day, all day, are my lover, mother, my best friend.
You know no limitations.
You shapeshift into my every want and need,
toast me with jam,
celebrate my awkwardness,
remind me of grace,

run your warmth all up and down the length of me
purring like a cat.
You kiss me repeatedly—
sun on back
rain on face
snow on eyelashes, a butterfly kiss.
You throw an arm around my shoulder, Day,
protect me like a shade tree.
I lean against the trunk of you when I'm afraid.
You say, "Listen I'm gonna be with you
all day today. Trust me,
you can have it all your way."

We act like puppies, yearlings, five-year-olds.
We roll on the ground with my dog,
weep with a friend on the phone,
sing to everything: a tree, my car, a plate I'm washing.
It's ridiculous I know, so
I blame it all on you.
You made me love you
even though it was not hard;
made me love your cutting chill
evening shadows
goose and whip-poor-will.
I loved you, glorious tricky Day,
even though you threw those curve balls
straight at me,
hollering, "Catch this!" way too late,
then laughing til the tears ran down your face.

When we lay down at last,
I felt your gentle weight press into me.
You were still chuckling at my antics

forcing me to say, "Hush you crazy Day.
Be quiet now. I need sleep."
You embrace me,
wrap me up in cozy memories,
then rock me as you make up fantasies
about your twin—
Tomorrow.

Baptism

The man in long black robes placed his right hand
on the bald head of his daughter.
Perhaps this was a bad idea.
Maybe a stranger would have made salvation
a little less personal, a little more probable.
But whatever else happened that day,
water did.
Water soaked into her soft spot,
ran down into round eyes the dark blue of deep Gulf,
dripped from her trembling chin
to soak the neck of her frilly white dress.
Lord, nobody ever told the preacher
how careful he need be
with that dip;
tiny round wafer in the head,
so vulnerable anything that touches it
sinks soul deep, stains the brain immortally.

Water at one month and she is sunk—
sinner and swimmer for life—
baptized in the name of the Water, the Sun, and the Holy Spritz,
without which she is bound to be a victim
of spontaneous human combustion.
Later, her father (baptizer of infant sprites),
is reminded of the danger
in which he left his unprotected daughter,
when she jumps into a motel pool in Waco,
and he must wet his best coat sleeve
reaching in to pull his toddler out
while she laughs with delight,

who just can't seem to get enough of this baptism thing.
Again in Sugarland,
she leaps without her floaty
into the deep end of the public pool,
sinks like a stone and stands
staring up at bare legs, smiling
at the sun, a bright yellow egg
floating on a pale blue plate of sky.
This time it's the lifeguard
who reaches his long, strong arm deep,
wrenching her to the surface smiling,
but he is stern enough to make her cry.
Finally, her parents decide that, no,
four is not too young for swimming lessons.
Thereafter, every time she had a cold or belly ache
or when the fear of polio was on them,
she stood beside the pool and wept,
Tiny Tears cradled to her small flat chest
waiting for the next pool day,
her whole body jonesing for the cool wet merging,
the moment water could again
wave across the once-soft spot
like it had that day from her daddy's hand;
a baptism that sank deep
saving her from flames.

Reflecting Paul

In that dusty Austin heat, he'd rock her
cradled close against his chest,
as he crooned his favorite Hank Snow songs—
they poured out of him like sweat;
mixing sweet with salty,
boy and baby's breath.
Her Momma, his big sister,
had agreed to let him stay
because there were too many kids at home
for their Dad's blue-collar pay.
No one had warned her Momma, yet,
beware young cowboys who mingle sweat
with innocence. Infants soak it like a sponge—
takes the place of mother's milk
and gets into their blood.
It shaped her features into his,
turned her restless dreamer.
Made her long for open spaces,
country music, women's faces,
created a lone cowgirl where
a Southern lady should have stood.
All that rocking to and fro
made her dream of riding
while sleeping in his arms.
Behind blue eyes lay miles
of blacktop she one day would roam,

a wagon wheel of spokes
from whatever hub she knew as home.

Pass the chicken. Pass the biscuits.
Pass the pepper, please.
On those hot Texas afternoons
Paul passed his salt to me.

Education

> *And if I have prophetic powers, and understand all mysteries and all knowledge, and if I have all faith, so as to remove mountains, but have not love, I am nothing.*
> —1 CORINTHIANS 13.2

> "Schooling is what happens inside the walls of the school, some of which is educational. Education happens everywhere, and it happens from the moment a child is born—and some say before—until it dies."
> —SARA LAWRENCE LIGHTFOOT

Thirty years ago I was thirteen and as new to the city
as bussing was to the bible belt.
Peaches and cream, country as an ear of corn
squeaky green to the ways of folk in a town called Jackson, Mississippi.
September saw me in my new school clothes
stiff as a mannequin suddenly humanized
and sent to Bailey Jr. High for punishment.
The school built by the WPA
was sprawling awkward ugly as a penitentiary
and I as hainty as a new prisoner can be.
New student blues in adolescence: Where to sit?
Who to talk to? How to move through a maze of rooms?
Where to eat and where to pee?
Where a friend in this sea of faces
for a girl who lacked in social graces?
Poor and proud, a preacher's kid
shooting through a growth spurt year
high-strung, sensitive, and queer . . .
though I didn't really know that, yet.
It just came off as "different."
Sand crab sidling to find somewhere in the middle—

someone to look up to,
someone to look down on.
That's how you fit in, right?
Along about that lonesome second week
my school was forced to integrate as they instigated
bussing to enforce the law which had been in place for years.

When their brown faces drifted in,
my social status shifted.
I was not the new kid anymore.
I could appreciate their fate, but realized too late
I shouldn't stare at her black hair, her velvet skin,
flashing eyes. Magnetized to defiance always
I adored the way she wore it to keep her safe
until she caught me looking and her anger and my fear
like flint and stone sparked hate.
Looks turned into words and words to sweat;
her vocabulary more adept at lashing out than mine,
I resorted to a tattler's threat—I'd "turn her in" for this.
She stared straight ahead, did not so much as blink an eye
and that's when I made the Big Mistake—
I touched her on the arm to make her look at me,
invading her last privacy. And that was it.
In the words that we used then, "the shit hit the fan"
and there was never any doubt about who was the shit
and who was the fan as she blew me totally away.
Dorothea Glass kicked my ass all the way across French class
rolling on the floor, through the door
her well-thrown punches thumping ripe against my bones.
We were to the stairs, her dark brown fingers
tangled in my straight blonde hair,
before two teachers broke it up at last.
They held her back, blowing that defiance through her fear

while I scrambled to my feet
the embarrassment of my weak tears wiped hard against my sleeve.
They separated us, sent us individually to see the principal.
Later on I looked for her but she was gone, sent home
expelled for three whole days while they let me stay.
I knew it wasn't right when all she'd done
was win the fight I started.

On the fourth day I stood waiting for her bus
trembling, skittish, scared 'cause she'd kicked my butt good once.
But I had a sense of fairness bigger than my pettiness
my ignorance and prejudice that kept me waiting there.
When she got off she took one look, hooked her fingers into fists
and praying, "Please God don't let her hit me first"
I walked forward, an apology forming on my lips.
I said, "I'm sorry that I touched you, hit you, looked too long.
I'm sorry you got sent home instead of me
just because you won the fight.
I'm sorry everything's unfair and, right now,
I'm sorry that I'm white."
Her arms relaxed, her fists unclenched
her face broke into the widest grin,
and like a boxer on TV, I reached out my hand.
Dorothea took it, shook it, and to her credit,
changed me.

A Dozen Ways of Looking at Thirteen

I

Jesus with his followers gathered for supper.
Judas enters, in his fist some coins,
on his lips a kiss.

II

The Knights Templar believed it would be
a Friday like any other in 1307.
They were wrong. Several saw heaven.

III

I ordered a dozen dinner rolls.
The bakery sent one extra.

IV

A woman who spells is a witch.
A woman who spells plus twelve is a coven.

V

A girl stares at the candles on her cake.
Will she go forward into her future
or run like hell back to childhood?

VI

The hangman coils a final turn into the noose.
A carpenter hammers the last step on the gallows.
The condemned man counts the minutes.

VII

Oh, Astronauts of Apollo, you
imagine walking on the moon.
The number of your mission
and an unforeseen explosion
will prove you're only dreaming.

VIII

For AA to work, you need
twelve steps and one desire to stop drinking.

IX

I threw the calendar away when
there were no more months.
There was still one moon left.

X

The boy becoming man holds the Talmud in his hand.
He grins beneath his yarmulke.
Today is his bar mitzvah.

XI

Six white stripes, seven red.
Steps on a pyramid. Olive branch, arrows,
stars overhead. Money and flag.
That's U.S. That's us.

XII

Missing: one floor in the building,
one aisle on the plane,

one room in the hallway,
can't trick me with 12-B—
triskaidekaphobia!

XII-B

How many ways are there to look at a blackbird,
Mr. Stevens?

Born Again

Nine hours of pool-watching
silver whistle flashing
lanyard looped around her neck
white string bright against brown skin.
Long hours wary guarding
shallow end to deep;
babies flapping water wings
to high school diving team.
This late August day a lashing rain,
the lifeguard's friend,
drove everyone away.
Now clouds thin to spots of blue, air cools
reminding her that school starts soon.
Eighteen and alone,
(other lifeguards long gone home)
bare-skinned but for two small strips of cloth,
"me Tarzan and me Jane."
She paces around the concrete cage.
Her heart pumps restlessly
as she examines her identity,
hears—animal . . . animal . . . animal.

Thirty-five yards of pool stretch
a magic aqua carpet at her feet.
No wave or splash now mars the perfect surface.
Smooth water seems so solid;
the door that opens, allows her in,

hidden in its skin.
She wishes her future looked like this.
There's nothing vague in water.
It's all about the clarity.
She strides toward the high board.
Ridged steel imprints her water-softened feet.
Each rung stretches calves, works tight thighs.
Muscles bunch her swimmer's shoulders,
twine down a rippling back.
She strides the requisite three steps
retracts one leg, a stork,
shoves into a heavy bounce,
up and out;
experiencing flight, or fall, or both—
jackknifes
straightens
plunges
into the deep blue follow-
through a door that's never locked.
She pulls an underwater length
as green trees blur edges of her vision.
The water warm compared to damp, cool air
gloves her body, its natural element.
Childhood dreams of breathing as she swims
return, an instinctual memory of gills
helps her power down the length of pool
emerging all elated,
bursting from the womb, oxygen-depleted
gasps for air;
from full immersion born again.

The Giving Tree

"I think that I shall never see a poem as lovely as a tree."
—JOYCE KILMER

That year, my first Christmas without:
without family
without gifts
without money, stocking, favorite foods—
was not without love.
I was in love for the first time,
and having discovered who I was,
had traded it for all that I held dear;
family, friends, church, and school.

We huddled in her living room
side-by-side on a well worn sofa
holding hands and sipping whiskey
to take away the ache of all I felt was missing:
relatives and congregation visiting the manse,
an open house—the centerpiece—our glittering tree.
No mom-wrapped presents waited there for me.
No smell of baking bread, pie, turkey, casserole or cookies.
My father, pretending I was non-existent,
insisted his family (and mine) do likewise.
No cards, letters, calls, or "came by 'cause I was in the neighborhood."
No cousins.

How can loneliness and love exist inside a single breast,
beating as they do, two different rhythms
on the drumskin of one heart?
Alone, together. Alone, together. Love, hurt. Love, hurt. Love . . .
rips the chest apart.

My lover's mother hid inside her room,
the muted sounds of television
emanating from the crack beneath the door.
Bottle clinked an empty glass
as she poured herself another scotch
to numb the recent loss of her drinking partner;
widowed for a month, lonely for a lifetime.
What she does now at Christmastime
is nothing new, is what she's always done.
My love grew up alone.
She didn't know to miss
the squealing of young children
the "ummm, ummm, ummm . . . " of hungry men
appreciating culinary artistry of wives;
the ripping of un-wrapping paper or
carols sung by people with good voices
who grew up knowing all the verses.
She never felt the heartmelt longing for the Christchild,
never even held a baby in her arms.
She was an only, lonely child
who won't miss the scent of evergreen,
the blink and twinkle of multi-colored lights,
the sharp flash of ornaments turning on the tree
as the sun goes down to merry night,
"Merry Christmas" night.
She's been an orphan all her life.
You cannot miss what you have never known.
I am all the love she owns.
It weighed on me; the guilt of wanting her to be enough,
to fill me up, to make the missing cease.
I could pretend, at least,
but not without a tree.

Late afternoon on Christmas Eve
a car pulled to the curb.
Not expecting anyone, we went out on the porch
to see a young man unfold himself from an old sedan
and step into the street.
He was over six feet tall, broad-shouldered,
handsome in his beard and jeans.
He looked at me until I recognized my brother in his eyes.
He'd been in the Navy. Two years
had passed since I saw him last.
He'd gained weight, muscle and good looks.
I hardly knew him.
He shook my hand and hers
as I introduced the two of them.
He wrestled with a tree he pulled out of the trunk.
Told me, "I didn't want you not to have one.
No one should be without a tree." He smiled,
carried it inside, not looking
at how drab a house can be
without a single decoration.
He set it in a stand he'd brought,
along with lights and ornaments.
In an hour he was gone
home to those who loved him,
never telling what he'd done.

Recently I heard a radio request for tales
about your favorite Christmas gift.
I only heard responses
from celebrities and the rich.
I wrote this piece for them because

really, aren't the best gifts things like these:
a hot meal when it's needed,
a little brotherly love,
a sweater you can give someone,
an unexpected Christmas tree?

Where is the Prince of Peace?

Where are you Prince of Peace?
We could really use you now and I keep seeing your followers
waving crosses, bibles, calling out your name
while they condemn lovers and activists alike
and refuse to let peace rest here.
We call ourselves Christians
but we take the name of the Lord in vain,
if you are truly the Prince of Peace.

Some people think of you stuck between the covers of a book
that's seldom really read, except for all the juicy parts;
a book everyone pretends to understand,
but who can know God's heart?
Others believe they've nailed you,
got you configured as the movie star you really are.
Now we can experience those final days in all their gory detail:
the floggings, stumbling beneath your cross toward Calvary,
crown of thorns, driving of the spikes—
renewing that old guilt of how we held the hammer.
But tell me, can all this really hold a candle
to what you watch humans do on a daily basis?
And isn't *that* what really hurts?

Christ, I don't believe you're hung up in lines of scripture
or the newest writer's script. We keep nailing you to a cross,
over and over . . .
but this is what touches us, brings the tear to our eyes.
Your physical suffering is long over.
Why is it you wring the compassion from us
who so easily ignore the starving children of the world

the tortured prisoners of war
women dying of breast cancer
millions dying of AIDS
and all of us choking on our own filth and carelessness.
All we have to do is stop, look, listen,
pay attention. There's suffering galore.

Oh, Prince of Peace
we look in all the wrong places . . .
inside churches, between the pages;
worshiping an empty cross we wait for your arrival
to avenge our personal vendettas
prove to everybody we were right
then float us up to heaven to gather round your feet
no matter how or even if
we practiced your beliefs.
Posturing Christians,
we don't know who you are, where you are
or what you may be doing.
We only know you're always on our side.

As for me, well,
I know how you come to me in my hour of despair.
I shut my eyes and you appear like magic
to me, who barely can believe in you.
And even though I tell you to get lost, go away
that you've never meant anything but trouble as far as I can see
you remain behind, speak softly so I can barely hear you
say "Be kind, be gentle, be fair, be just."
"Be at peace, child; be peace."
I succumb to the hum of your voice, and weeping
am allowed to see how many places you can be at once
as you walk barefoot among the wounded:

There you are in the cancer ward of Grady Memorial Hospital
where only the poorest go,
and there in Iraq as you comfort some civilian who's lost his legs.
You're blessing the weddings of San Francisco queers
forgiving the preacher who still wants to kill poor Matthew
though he's been dead for years.
There you are out there doing that thing I cannot believe,
will never achieve,
loving each and every one the same.

Who knows better than you, Prince of Peace,
torture is nothing new.
There are a thousand ways to hang someone on a cross
and we've explored them all.
What's hard, what's really tough is lifting up the fallen,
forgiving your tormentors,
refusing to take from those who can't defend themselves.
We each must do what's hardest and what's hard is
holding the one you hate in your arms stinking and bleeding
carrying him to safety, bathing his wounds
healing him and yes, saying we're sorry
for how long we have ignored, or even caused, his suffering.

Clothe the naked. Feed the hungry. Heal the sick.
If we dedicate our lives to this
(as was suggested)
there would be no time for war.
Where are you Prince of Peace?

How many times Lord should I forgive?
Once? Three times? Seven? How many times to get me into heaven?
He said, "Seventy times seven." 490; that's a lot.
He said "Turn the other cheek."
He said, "Love your enemies" because that's harder than your friends,

most times.
This is no vengeful God come to taste the fruits of retribution.
This here's the Son of God,
big idealistic dreamer with a soft spot for down-and-outers
imploring us to love each other and learn how to forgive
reminding us, it's the only way to live.

Where is the Prince of Peace?
He's caged behind the ribs of humankind
(that's you and me)
where the heart of him beats rhythmically, repeatedly
"love each other, love each other, love each other."

It's up to us to set Him free.

Before You Jump

For Meagan

She stands firm in a big old Birch.
Its limbs stretch over the same length of river
her granddad swam when he was just a kid.
She is just a kid herself, rangy as a boy;
her thick brown hair pulled into a ponytail
shows off her pixie features, the brown shells of her ears.
Her face gazes at something no one else can see,
some future far away as college
or closer than the swirling water
flowing past beneath her.
She waits for her courage to catch up
to how fast she can climb, stand alone,
take hold of the rope.
Nearly breathless, she considers how her feet
will leave the sureness of the branch and then . . .
What happens next?
She can only guess.
There are so many firsts for a girl
green as the leaves which frame her
and she will not be rushed.
No "Ready-set-go!" or "Jump!" will make her leave her perch.
This girl knows her mind.
What happens next?
We are left to guess.

Thoughts zip past like swallows dip and dive
touch the water, fly.
She is not a swallow, though.
Flight depends on courage, heart,

her willingness to risk
adventure.
Shoulders arch wings, aching to be tried.
Thin brown feet shift.
What she can't yet know, she can anticipate:
rush of wind, the muddy water taste,
mouth full of sunshine as she swings
from beneath the canopy of leaves,
body suspended in mid-air when she lets go
as the rope releases her from all she's ever known.
Momentum, once begun,
will take us somewhere.
That's for sure.

This flight, with all its fear and fascination,
will only be first once.
What she appears to know right now
(how quickly we forget)
is not to rush the moment, let it linger.
Stand a moment in that place where you're familiar
with the feel of everything.
Appreciate your apprehension.
Realize you'll never be the same.
Know with every act we're changed.

Then my girl, let fly and take it in;
all the highs and lows
the swing the fall
the grace that lands us on our feet
or sinks us deep in Mystery
the breath that brings us back
the Self that, if we let it, always rises up to meet
both our victories and defeats.

Remind us how time passes fast
and how much more we need to be
open and alive as this young girl
poised in the widespread arms of a tree,
life flowing past beneath our feet.

Revival

> *Except you become as a little child, you shall not enter the kingdom of heaven.*
> *For whosoever humbles himself as a child shall be greatest in the kingdom of God.*
>
> —MATTHEW 18.3–4

In the dimness of churchlight at night
she sits and sniffs at dusty hymnals.
Too young yet for pimples,
she picks a scab on her right knee until it bleeds.

"Only His blood can wash you clean!"

Six days of spiritual scrubbing
and still her soul lies limp in her belly
wrinkled and dirty as a soiled pair of panties
at the bottom of the laundry basket.

"Repent, and be saved from eternal damnation!"

Her sins hover over her,
drawn like dark moths to the light of her brief life.
Afflicted fairies, they flutter and dance behind closed lids.
Neck bent in prayer, she dares not lift her head
for fear of Daddy's glare from the pulpit.
So she studies the open sore
pretends hard it's bullet hole
and she's a wounded cowboy and not
the only unsaved soul amongst a bevy of believers.
Head down, she avoids the frown she knows
is tugging at the corner of her mother's mouth
where she sits beside her.

"Imagine my friends what hell is like!"

She can, but doesn't want to.
And while words of fire flame from the face
that with a whiskery trace, graces her room at bedtime
and the same sweet lips that kiss her cheek to sleep
grimace with damnation while the congregation groans,
she taps the toes of her Mary Janes,
wishing she was home
or playing on the grassy knoll behind the church
at kick-the-can or hide-and-seek
or catching fireflies to be released,
the crushed ones glowing on her fingertips—
to her, a good example of what can happen
when you let your little light shine bright.
She swallows all her dad's descriptions
like her mother's bitter health prescriptions,
expecting dreams of screaming folks, who
once boasting disbelief,
stand roasting in red-yellow heat
no green to cool their burning feet
a fate she knows awaits her.
Awake late, the sheets bind her in a starchy knot,
the sweat of future fires makes her hot
and she tries not to sleep, but does
and dreams:

She's in her own backyard. It's Spring.
Mimosas bloom a frilly pink
and honeysuckle hangs, its summery perfume
fills up all the room inside her
as she gazes at the mitt on her left hand,

a softball glowing whitely in the trap.
She has on jeans and hightops,
a t-shirt that says Jesus Shops at K-Mart and SAVES.
She's not sure exactly what it means
but accepts it (like we do in dreams)
and looking up sees the Son of God Himself
looking hopefully at her.
He wears the flowing robes and curling hair
she's seen in pictures everywhere
but his eyes seem neither sad nor mad.
In fact, He's smiling and she assumes He's glad
He's got a softball glove on his hand, too.
She's not quite sure what she should do
but He punches His mitt like a pro, calls out
"C'mon and throw!"
She grips the ball and pitches,
hopes like hell that He won't miss it.
He snags it easily, throws back
a perfect toss she catches a little to one side.
That's when she discovers something has rubbed off
on the globe of bleached cowhide;
because the ball that's nestled in her glove
—is full of Love.
How else to explain it;
that warms her mitt and fills her hand
reaches up the length of arm to bleed into her chest
until her entire body shines with its powerful radiance.
Overcome, she feels too young
to understand this kind of love,
but knows she can appreciate
what is good and kind and whole.

In that twilit world the two play catch
and every time she throws it smack! into His mitt,
she hopes He feels her love Him back.
They don't talk.
The ball expresses all they have to say
and they play until the day discovers her in bed,
when just before His last pitch finds her glove,
the ball becomes a dove and flies away.

Blood

The Straight Dope

> *Then Jesus said to him, "Put your sword back into its place; for all who take the sword will perish by the sword.*
> —MATTHEW 26.52

Sunday afternoon in Red Oak Project
I ride through in blue, my favorite color blue
the uniform, the cop car blue
my mood blue as a bruise going gray.
I look at the folks who people my beat
for the most part they are black.
They do not call themselves African-American
nor do we when we rattle off descriptions on the radio:
"Be on the lookout for a black male
(dark-skinned, brown-skinned, light-skinned) male,
18 years of age, fade cut, green shirt, purple baseball cap."
How many times have I heard that endless repetition?
Blue with it, I watch their quiet desperation
stare at me from doorsteps, glaring menace
sleepy, dope-stained whites of eyes
to wide-eyed innocence.
I want to follow them into the haze—
they think I don't know but I do.
They think I don't care but I do.
They think I don't go there. I do.
Down corridors of weaving walls
crawling through never-ending halls
of blurring color where everything,
every thing feels just right in that good night
mushy-cushy thick dark doughy world of dope.
I want to park my cruiser at the door of 1–5-3
walk up on the porch

remove my vest, strip down to my tee
find a spot of sun, sit back and take a hit
then talk some jive ass shit
that no one gives a damn about
our voices droning on and on,
the buzz of bees at happy flowers.
Yeah, that's what I want.
But I don't. I never do.
Nobody knows what I do with all those hours.
I ain't out front porch sittin.'
I'm slitting my wrists slowly.
I hide behind my badge and dose my dope so carefully
sparingly, a little at a time,
just enough to see me through:
the next two foot chases where all I can retrieve
is this piece of crap, this purple hat;
the next domestic where she requires stitches
but still she won't press charges;
four burglaries, a heart attack,
three accidents, one drunk
and a long trip to the county jail
madman in the back who calls me bitch and lezzie
and sends my ass to hell with every other breath.
Just enough to get me back to Red Oak in the rain
enough to dull the pain of watching as the water stains
a "black male's" shirt and pants
he, not even sixteen yet, stabbed
ice pick in the back
over some lousy crack and fifty bucks.
Enough to fight off shocked relations 'cause
"What we've got here is a crime scene, folks."
Enough to stand the strain of waiting
because it's Sunday and it's raining

and the ambulance don't fly
and homicide won't ride on Sunday in the rain.
Hours pass. His people wail
and I want to open up and howl with them
but I'm too cool dressed all in blue
with the sergeant stuck beside me
making jokes so sick I swear I'll beat him
with my stick before I listen to another one.
The boy's auntie yells, "Do something!"
And I want to.
I want to gather his thin body in my arms
hold him to my chest and rock him there for all to see
and weep for him and her and me.
But I don't. I never do.
I pull the haze down lower so it covers both my ears
stuff back the tears and watch his body silently
watch as his identity turns soggy first
then fades, finds the drain
and washes pinkly out to sea.
Don't get me wrong. I don't do much. Just enough
to take care of me.

How Love Changes the World

for Catherine and Mara's wedding

This boy, maybe twelve, has a spot on a nearby hill
where he hides when the pressures of his day become too much to bear:
when his stepfather curses him for leaving the dirty glass or uncut grass
on his list of things to do tomorrow
or hits him with an open fist for being late to supper
as his mother lights another cigarette and the smell of beer and liquor
soaks the air like gasoline until he's afraid the Bic she clicks
may burn their house to smoking ashes.
When, on any given evening,
parental voices rise like the caws of angry crows
and discord scrapes his sensitive ears,
he runs to his hiding place
here, night watchman, this boy sits alone.
From his bunk beneath a spreading hemlock where he lies
with green sighs of breeze and the comfort of its spicy breath
sucked between his lips,
the boy can see the cottage
kitchen window with a lemon-yellow glow
never curtained like the rest,
the light a square of blessing to the darkened earth below.
He watches as the women through the window cook their supper
sees the way they touch each other
knows the talk at school, at home, in town
knows his mother won't let him mow their lawn.
The words like battering rams assault him here
names like dykes, daggers, queers
but the term that simply will not fit the silent scene
is the word "unnatural"
because what he sees on his private tv screen

seems like the most natural thing this boy has ever seen.
At his silent picture show he sees the two,
one with blond hair one with brown,
touch heads as they look together through a book
a cookbook he supposes,
faces frown, heads shake, hands upturn
or gesture toward the cabinets
until finally they light on one which must be the right one
for they nod and smile and crease the book in place.
They hug (as if the discovery of some recipe were equal to a foreign land)
or the blond kisses the cheek of the brunette
as the brunette rises and begins to gather items
for the stew or casserole or salad
then leans to plant a kiss in the blonde one's hair
which he imagines nests there like a sparrow.
He watches while they prepare their meal and wonders
at how everything they touch seems treated with such love.
He wishes anyone would put their hands on him as tenderly
as the dark haired woman lifts a canister of flour.
He pretends when they embrace that he stands between them
their arms wrapping him in live wires,
their love for one another flowing like a current
through his body until he is charged for life.
This boy adores it when their heads fall back
their mouths wide and smiling;
in the summer their laughter cascading
from the screen in a pretty waterfall of sound.
In the year since he's been coming here
he's seen them serious and sad—both have cried—
he doesn't know why but he saw one take a wadded napkin
from the table once and wipe her tears away.
He has seen them kiss and doesn't turn away from this
but studies how they linger,

fingers brushing cheeks and hair and lips
as if this were all the education he would ever need
and just this once he'd like to make an A.
This boy is not "grossed out."
On the contrary he collects their kisses
as he does his special treasures;
river rocks and feathers placed in his bottom drawer
where he studies them with pleasure late at night when he's alone.
This boy is in love with them.
He wants to marry them.
He does not want to marry someone like his mother.
He does not want to be his father or his grandfather.
He doesn't want to be the boys at school who call the women names
making fun of what they can't begin to understand.
If he ever loves a woman—and he wants to and he will—
he wants to love a woman the way they love each other.
He hopes to make this cozy kitchen scene his own
when he will help her choose the meal and cook it
and they will touch and talk and laugh the way these women do
hands held before they eat thanking God and one another
for all that they've been given.
He will stand beside her at the sink the way they're doing now;
she washing, he drying with a checkered towel
facing out toward the darkness through a window with no shade
shoulders touching, unafraid of being seen
by lonely boys like him.
This the picture he takes with him, tucked like a beloved
photo in the back pocket of his mind;
the one he would show everyone,
pointing proudly to these women, claiming to his friends,
"When I grow up I want to be like them."

Ode to the Dark

for a friend in surgery

This time, let the dark take you down.
Bed down soft as a feather pillow,
your head velvet in its embrace.
Give yourself to the dark;
pinpoints of light, of consciousness dimming
until the dark has substance.
Once I felt the dark like a big, black dog
rub its fur along my leg.
I wanted to call it back,
know the difference between its eyes and tail.
(It's wagging now,
laughing that there is no difference—
in the dark.)
Let the dark stroke the length of you;
hold your hand, your head, cradle your body.
Believe there are times when it's better not to see.
This time the darkness is your friend.
It is the cave of our caring, the womb of our love.
Let it rock you.
When next we see you, drowsy
and clinging to those last black crumbs,
our hands will bring you back—
stroke your cheek with whispers,
lead you gently to the light, slow as sunrise.
Not too much at first,
dark only seconds away,
quick escape until you're ready
for the full light of healing to begin.

Death in the Holler

It was a killing kind of day.
The path that needed to be cut
chopped with machete and swing blade by hand
left a swath of withered saplings
crippled grasses, strangling ivy
trampled down and then
the moths and bees and flies
that liked to enter in
through all the screenless windows
and then there were the fish
we caught in tandem: one, two, three
just when it seemed they wouldn't bite,
big bass I'd thrown on ice,
their deaths less glory by a numbing sleep
than by decapitation.
Now I was born to fishing
and have been cleaning them since my first catch
but the years have made me kinder
(or some would say more stupid)
to attribute feelings to a fish.
I only keep the biggest ones
because I have a taste for bass fried Southern style
that still outweighs my consciousness.

Back at the cabin I began to clear the porch
which had become a minefield in my absence,
of every kind of winging, stinging Nazi bug
that ever crept from comb or cone
to stick its stinger somewhere soft
like back of thigh or under arm.

I'd spray and run and spray and run
until I reached the hornets' nest,
a tougher fortress by far than wasps' open air retreats.
Carefully constructed to keep all killers out
perfect hole in paper-mâché
I sprayed and sprayed and sprayed
then ducked inside and looked to see;
a friend kept watch beside me.
They buzzed with wrathful indignation that faded to a drone,
but they were hard as hell to kill
even for an executioner come creeping in their sleep
converting nests to gas chambers,
making tombs out of their combs.
Darkness dropped a shade of gray.
It was curtains for them all.

I was relieved the day was done.
I had my scars:
rash of poison ivy itches, a sting on upper thigh,
the fin cuts on my hands clotted full of grit.
I'd combated nature long enough,
I thought, clear the loft and quit.
I took the stair above the landing with left foot
right foot poised above its head
primal fear rush so innate I pivoted and fled.
"Get down! Hurry up, get down from there!"
was all I'd time to say.
Right quick she was beside me,
"Holy shit," she said.
There he was, a lariat, coiled loosely on the step
as if some careless cowboy
left it laying looped about
before heading up to bed.
Now I knew that snake and I were on a time-share plan

but we'd agreed we'd never see each other anytime.
He'd honored our agreement with calling cards of skin
thinly wrapped about the chairs or
draped along the stairs,
sometimes wisping in the breeze
along the porch or from the trees
but never in these two years
had I come face to face with him, nor with the fear of him
in this familiar place.
I never dreamed he'd be so big,
so shiny black, so alien,
eight feet at least at his full length,
lay coiled upon the stair.
My friends who said "don't kill them"
well, none of them were there.
They'd say, "Get a rake and put him out"
but the only way was toward us.
I couldn't help but wonder
what eight black writhing feet of belt
would feel like round my waist.

"We'll never sleep again, my friend,
if we don't kill him now.
Even if we get him out, he's sure to come back in."
I listened to the truth in that, got my snub-nose .38.
Not knowing how much killing power
a snake that big would take,
I loaded it with smaller rounds and found a spot to brace.
At first I felt the strength of that old adrenaline pump.
I would not leave my house for him
or find him here alone
hanging from the rafters or curled up on my throne.
I watched his flickering tongue
test air, taste fear—

what finally made him come?
Was it out of curiosity or to offer us a greeting?
Or to stake a claim in this his house
or was it just the beating of the air
made by dying hornets' wings?
I drew a bead, ignoring his bad timing
with steady hand I squeezed
and knew that I had hit the target.
But the rounds were old, had gotten wet,
the gun misfired, had no effect,
popped like some dud firework, gun smoke acrid in the air.
The three of us just stared.
He looked alarmed but didn't move while my resolve
dissolved, insubstantial as champagne
too long upon the tongue.
I did not want to kill him then.
But there's an urgency in wrongness that refuses to be righted
and I fired again.
Another miss, another curse,
half-hearted measures, surely worse
than the sudden kiss of death.
The fourth shot found his middle.
Slammed against the wall by force,
I was sure that he was dead, but no,
no, not at all; he lifted up his head,
stretched his body upward so we could see his beauty
scattered in the snow-white underbelly
black ink blots in fine chaotic patterns.
Opening his mouth, he screamed out his betrayal,
his pain, his bewilderment,
at this strange turn of events.
He howled into the void that yawned endlessly before him,
noiseless, soundless screams, begging me to end it
but I couldn't for the life of me,

not even for the death of him,
fire that final round.

I begged, "You have to finish him"
and showed her with a shovel.
She tried it first out on the porch to gather up her courage,
while we two in our wretchedness
shared every silent scream
and my heart flooded through my chest
where I had broken it.
She reappeared before me, her face as hard as it can get
her hands screwed tight around the shaft
"Don't think, just do it" and she did.
I found a box and she raked his broken body down.
I stood trembling with remorse, frozen by my shame
stuck inside a photograph,
sad still-life,
freeze-frame.
I simply stood
looked at the blood
as red as yours or mine, that salty source of life
that links us all now wasted on the stairs.
How could I ever justify killing something out of fear?
I'd tried to carve a space for me to think, to write, to be alone.
Safety don't come easy.
It's hard to make a home.
He was there first, I knew, but humanity won out
with money, poison, and a gun
I'd taken everything he owned.
The one thing that he left behind
was the judgment stamped within
that in my forty years of life
I'd done more harm than him.

Dress Blues

Cotton underwear soft against skin
Polyester blue, shined black boots
Badge, nametag, bright silver buttons
Webbed leather gunbelt, radio mute.

Long, slick baton through a black plastic hole
Freshly oiled handcuffs behind on one hip
Cold steel Beretta's right angle to sole
Snug in a holster, beside it two clips.

High on the ankle a short .38
Cylindered hollowpoints five shots extra
Four chambered shells behind a Winchester plate
Of a shotgun, a safety, a chest Kevlar-vested.

Clipboard, report forms, pen with black ink
Wrinkled bag lunch in the passenger seat.

Opera Light

For Pete, Chris, and Andrea Bocelli

Every afternoon around 1 P.M.
she watches the same opera DVD
of a famous young tenor.
I see him on the screen as I pass through for tools,
paint, caulk, patch and primer.
He is Italian handsome, olive-skinned,
with a four-day growth of beard,
wearing black and white,
dark on light,
sun and shadow.
His voice soars through all the rooms and out
across the lake in pure tones —
an alabaster bird emerging from a cavern,
unexpected and brilliant.

I don't know the tenor's name
but I'm told he's blind.
He can't see the Tuscan light, the fields,
only feel the fiery sun against his face.
He can't see how his father looked
holding out his boyhood hand to the pump,
only feel the cold well up between his fingers
hearing tones in the water
his father can't imagine.

At first I don't understand what she finds to comfort her
in this opera ritual, these repeated arias.
But as the days slip by, something sweet is growing

inside my own particular gloom;
something bright as the smile that breaks across the tenor's face
at the thunderous applause,
a bar of sunlight through blinds.
Yet her face remains a mask, unreadable.

And what initially I dreaded I now await,
watching the clock, anticipating his call;
the untranslatable libretto echoing through
the heart's chambers, giving rise to dreams
that otherwise would remain
locked away somewhere
in the dark.

Seeds

for Rachel Corrie

When I was a little girl Momma taught me how to plant a garden.
"Hold your hands like evening prayers and open up the top."
Then she would furrow seeds in between my folded palms.
"Now go down the row, let the seeds fall
one by one into the crumbled soil
and pray for them to grow."

This, too, is how you sow peace . . . faith . . . love.
Put your palms together, pray.
Plant little seeds everywhere you go.
Where the soil is rocky, gently
move the stones aside or simply plant around them.
Where the plot is overgrown
pull the weeds and recycle in the compost;
eventually they will turn to dirt again.
When the ground is frozen
lay down and warm it with your body
or like Rachel Corrie,
thaw it with your blood.
Don't give up
even if some seeds are wasted, lost
or fall on poisoned ground.
Growth is never-ending work.
Tend your garden and also plant your neighbor's.
There is joy in caring for innocent beings.
There is exaltation in the harvest.
There is celebration when everyone is feasting.
Faith . . . love . . . peace . . .
food for life.

Now put your palms together, pray.

Burst of Light: A Tribute to Audre Lorde

> *"When I dare to be powerful—to use my strength in the service of my vision, then it becomes less and less important whether I am afraid."*
>
> —AUDRE LORDE

She comes to me in spirit rags
blacker than her skin
comes ghosting into the study where I write
one night late to frighten me.
She's too large for this small space
everything about her big and dark as after-midnight
with stars for eyes and teeth of gleaming ivory.
She laughs at my dropped jaw,
whistles low as a cold north wind
sprung suddenly through my open window.

"Audre . . . Audre Lorde?
But you're . . . you're dead."

"Child, tell me something I don't know."
Her robe falls open like a curtain parting
exposing jagged scars, a flat-scraped chest,
the once-a-woman's-now-girl's breast,
her scarlet heart beating like a jimbe drum.
Some voodoo muse has brought her here.
Open wounds are everywhere.
I close my eyes so I don't have to see.
"Gone but not forgotten, that's me.
No, don't turn your head. Look at me.
I may seem a little raggedy, but then again
you'll look like this one day.
You don't get through life without some scars

and you're barely getting started."
She raises her arms, a gospel preacher.
"You got to be brave, girl. Listen here. I'll teach you.

Never be afraid to be the first at anything,
or be afraid but be first anyway.
Somebody's got to lead.
You know most folks are followers.
They'll do it, too, if you show the way—
but you've got to get the ball to rolling
before it picks up any speed.
Who'll take the risk that starts momentum?
You satisfy that need.
Don't come cryin' to me,
'It's too hard. I'm not the one. Let some younger body do it.'
I know hard, believe you me,
black, lesbian, mother, warrior, poet.
My seed was planted and grown to maturity
through the '40s and the '50s.
Why, my skin alone made me hard to see.
But then I had to go and be a lesbian
getting busted for this dream I had
that we're all just human beings.
Losing my identity became a way of life
colored girl among the dykes
outcast from my race and culture
until I discovered that repeating who I am
over and over and over
would make me true to my own nature:
Black lesbian mother poet warrior.

Young, I was so angry swaggering in my flannel shirts and jeans
but I mellowed as I aged into the softer-spoken
deeper-thinking, dashiki-wearing dyke

I eventually became.
I honed my sword on the grindstone of my poetry
and made the reader feel the blade I learned to wield
against ignorance and poverty, racism, sexism, hate
because I couldn't hold all that ache inside.
Then fighting cancer took my time
losing first my left breast, then my right.
Uh-huh, I wrote the book on pain.
The *Cancer Journals;* they're the proof
some hells,
like loss and hurt,
can grow to be your greatest work.

I refused their prosthesis,
horrified my nurse and counselors.
I said, How will people know what happened to me?
What's happened to all the others?
What's happening every day?
There are so many women suffering
but nobody's gonna know if we put on plastic make-believes,
act like this ain't happening to you and you and me.
I want a million topless women marching to the White House
so the powers that be can see this long line of chests
flat and scarred from hazardous wastes
until ten million women's voices shout,
'Look at us, see our scars! We demand you
stop the wars you wage on women's bodies.
Stop smoking up the atmosphere
so there's death in every breath.
Stop selling us your tainted food.
Stop poisoning our water.
Here are your strip mines,
your mountain top removals—

what's left across our chests.'
Survivors, get tattoos of fire-breathing dragons
and widespread trees where
your beautiful breasts should be.
Don't be afraid to draw attention to what our nation will not see.
Whose shame is this?
It's not us who've lost our dignity.

I guess that's it. My time is up. I've said what I came to say.
Now write it down and tell the women this for me:
Your dreams are more important than your fears.
Your passion counts more than your time here
and the most important thing you'll leave behind
is the legacy of your own life.
Remember, only what you love will last."

Audre spread her cape then, which opened into night,
left me standing breathless in a blinding burst of light.

Touch Wood

    for Cheryl

The day after you died, I worked hard
searching out wood left over from the storm.
Riding a mower, dragging a wagon
I thought about that summer day
I saw you astride your tractor in the orchard
as we passed you on the way to the river.
I told Path "back up" because I saw you
making gestures I'd been taught
were those of someone about to have a heart attack.
Your craggy face was pale as a ghost's
driving a slow mower into the Elysian Fields of Forever.
You were simply annoyed I made you cut the engine,
and I knew I'd breached some bad butch rule
about worrying too much, still
I accepted your slight scorn because I cared,
cared about what happened to you.

The day after you died I drove the mower slow,
smoked a doobie in your honor,
uncovered piles of wood dotting my 3 acres,
loaded it, drove it to the growing hill up near the house,
dumped it, did it all again.
It was so cold I had to beat the logs
which lay frozen to the ground.
It was gray, a real winter day.
That was good. It matched my mood.
Besides, I could see you better
with a backdrop not so bright.
How many times had you touched wood
to load a stack or split it with an axe
in order to keep warm, keep the fire burning

on the hearth, in the muscles, in the heart?
I felt you strengthen me as I hefted up the splitter,
rose to my toes to make that little jump
which brings the blade down hard enough
to pop a length of stove wood with a single stroke.

The day after you died, this is what I did, all day.
This is what I do when sorrow strikes.
When I feel loss, I work the body hard,
wearing out the restlessness; the tears
can come unnoticed, the sobs an engine sound
throbbing through the forest, up the path toward home.
With every log I rolled or split or lifted
you were with me.
And since I never knew
the last time I saw you would be the last time,
I named that day, the day after you died,
the Last Time because I saw you
in the faces of the wood I hauled
to feed the stove that makes the blaze
that cheers a cold, dark Ozark night.

That evening, the day I now last saw you,
I stood beneath the backyard pine
and touched a limb still sticky with sap
startling a small bird
who flew from her hiding spot
in a thick green knot of needles.
I felt a little hope to see her there,
to feel her wings just brush my hair,
and I promised then
I would not touch wood again
without some small remembrance of you;
remembering, too, that touching wood
is suppose to bring good luck.

There is no moral to the story

The dead limb didn't look
like a diving board at first.
The tree seemed lifeless
but as April greened to May
thin teardrops of locust leaf dripped
from its arthritic fingers
and that gnarled and ugly column
became central to the day.
On Sunday a storm blue with thunderheads
boiled in from distant peaks.
The wind took a deep breath
and exhaled into the trees
like a kid with candles on a birthday cake
and just one wish,
to blow.

There . . .
the turbulent curtain of smoky gray
parts, unveils two ravens in silhouette
against a sky in chaos.
They do not seem to care
the world is coming to an end.

There is . . .
no doubt, some non-anthropomorphic reason
for their meeting at this precarious place
above a sea of windy emptiness,
black feathers sleek as '50s greasers
cruising for a Saturday night street fight.
They are surfers daring hurricanes in wetsuits
waiting for the biggest wave to coil and break;

one final breath-defying ride before retiring to some cave.
There must be some sane reason
for leaving the security of nests
to leap into a gale-rocked universe
without the use of safety nets.

There is no . . .
grasping their behavior as they stand
one behind the other on the limb;
greasy feathers lifting in the gusts,
turning yet again to stare
at one another, offering a silent dare.
The first one tips his head, top hat
to wind, one eye cocked,
he estimates the drop.
Amazing, how the slightness of his weight
keeps him balanced in one place.
Clouds shoot straight up, meet a horizontal blow
with all the scary force of Dorothy's tornado.
The diver finds his stance,
hesitates, counts one
before he takes the plunge;
hurls his birdy body off
pushed down by hands
that weight him like an albatross,
then he's updrafted and across,
wings beaten back by wind.

There is no moral . . .
hesitation in the second bird;
no consideration that life might be too precious
to wager soul on such a careless throw of dice.
Braver, having watched his companion catch the wind,
he dives and barrel-rolls, following his friend

into that early morning night until, he, too
is irretrievably snatched from sight.

What compelled them to this crazy stunt?
That same force which pushed me to a stony ledge
skinny adolescent arms and legs hanging fire above
the faraway green water of abandoned gravel pit?
And made me jump . . .
flapping arms recalling wings long since evolved past flight.
Must I feel myself what it means to freefall forty feet?
Or was it the attraction of the stillness
right before that singular half-step
from which there is no turning back?
The perfect lonely place of pounding heart
and quickened breath;
the silence of the second that seems to precede violence
when the body tells the brain it's committed, to commence.
How cool the gulp of blessed air before Lucifer talked back.
The clean sea taste of spit as Eve's tongue touched the apple.
The sweet tenderness that pained him as Judas bent to kiss.

There is no moral to the . . .
common language between wind and bird and raw-boned girl.
A friend fancies that dogs are making music
in wee hours of the morning
when city creatures howl their common language out
to ululate above the cyclone fence in voices
which refuse their pens and rise above the dog food dishes
to sink their teeth in flesh and bone
and roam the darkened earth alone
until they leap beyond their senses,
singing
that eternity is glimpsed
the moment just before the fall.

Subtraction

The Pentagon can't count in single digits.
If they could, they would know that
at the rate of 2 per day,
we lose 14 soldiers every week;
that's 56 lives a month,
672 men and women a year.
Nearly 7,000 sons and daughters dead already
with the war not over yet.
Seems Washington can only count in millions and billions.
Numbers in the hundreds, even thousands
are lost on them.
They deal in multiple gains, not losses.
Congress has never learned to subtract.

Here's a math lesson for you:

A 19-year-old boy sits with his small unit
in an armored car on the edge of an Afghan village,
on the edge of his seat, on edge period
because last night insurgents blew up his buddy's group
where they guarded boundaries
with night goggles, M-16s, and hand grenades
none of which did them any good.
This is Al Qaeda country,
nothing like North Carolina.
It makes him think about that funny picture
called "Indians in the Desert" where all
that's visible are cactus, sand and rocks.

His buddy is dead, along with 2 others.
Just last week the 2 of them

drank beer and half-drunk
played volleyball in the sand.
The sweat pops on his forehead
to think he might be next.
Night after night he waits and wonders
who will die tonight?
He wants to go home now.
His tour is young yet—he has 10 months
to wait and wonder.
300 nights
to become a single-digit statistic
in a war that should be over
in a land where he's suppose to fight for freedom,
tho' nobody here, not even he, seems free to him.

At home in the hills
his mother waits and wonders
if her fair-haired son will make it home
to eat the corn she shucks to freeze for winter
the tomatoes and green beans she's grown and canned.
She likes to think of him tanned and tow-headed
picking tobacco from the back of his daddy's tractor.
Was that just last year?
She lies awake all night
keeping the watch with her only son, forgetful
that their time is not the same.
She knows the dark is dangerous.
She stares at the green hands of her bedside clock
as they tick off 1, 2, 3 minutes—
she knows this is how many Americans die in Afghanistan
daily. Even she can count how many that will be
by the time his tour is done.
She knows the number 1
is all it takes to lose and ruin

more lives—hers, his father's, his 2 sisters',
his grandmother's.

When she voted for this president,
she believed he could add and subtract.
She thought he could count
but she is bitter to realize he's limited to dollars,
not sense, and now her son's life
ain't worth a plug nickel up in Washington.
She, however, can subtract,
has had to cut some losses,
and this is more than the sum of all of them.
She knows enough to be afraid.
She wants her son home to eat her cooking,
swim in the South Toe River
court the country girl who loves him
lie safe in his own bed dreaming
the dreams of peaceful sleepers—
not watching, waiting, wondering if the night
will demand his 1 and only life.

Iraq/Afghanistan War Heroes Dot Com

(www.iraqwarheroes.com)

I feel I owe it to my country to check this site—
as a veteran, a concerned citizen.
I need to know the names of the "fallen,"
euphemism for being blown to bits
gut shot, broke-brained.
I need to see the faces of these people
who believe they are doing this for me.
And believe me, I believe they believe.
If not, they will be convinced:
after a few gory films in basic training
after hearing the word *enemy* said
side by side with *towel-head* countless times,
indeed, once they've visited this site.

I wasn't looking for you, Tracy Alger,
but your smile was ablaze in your face,
your tan jaw stubborn and strong.
It seems I recognized my soldier self
from so many years ago.
I clicked in to see your story:
Wisconsin gal who loved horses,
Mom and Country;
a woman who couldn't stand to see a matinee
in the middle of a sunny day.
You lived for the deep green breaths of summer,
never could be corralled inside a kitchen,
felt stuck in your own studio.
You twitched inside a nurse's scrubs.
Every minute inside a house
was a minute more staring through an open window

looking for a way back out.
And you found one.
You seriously considered it,
thought it over long and hard until
the time that you spent barrel racing
made you feel your valor must be tested.
Muscled thighs hugged your pony like a lover,
one with his stride, his twist your twist,
right—left—right
until the cadence in the drum of Tango's hooves
reminded you that Duty called.
No desk for you, no;
only Airborne Assault would do.
Was it lonely to be one of "the brave, the proud,
the few" women?
You graduated in March of 2007,
shipped out in April, maybe May.
A six-month stay and your life was over
by the first day of November.

Lovely, hard-bodied warrior lost at thirty
to a gold bar and a short ride in a real humvee.
There are no soft edges to a bronze star
clenched in a mother's hand.
A purple heart can't beat, can't love
can't sit astride a pony.
Some will say you should not have gone,
your finger should never have itched
to twitch the trigger of that M4.
But I know how the little "perfect marksman" rifle
felt pinned over your left pocket
where all the men could see.
The warrior must have her war.

Your last trip home was in a flag-draped box
and all that's left of you is in the broken
faces of your sister, mother;
in Tango's empty, hanging tack.
No mention of a husband, or a lover.
If that lover is a she
there will be no mention,
no recognition, no Army pension
to help her muddle through her misery.
No matter, Hero,
may you receive your just rewards.
On that All Souls Day
I hope the saints lined up to greet you,
saluted as you walked a gauntlet of respect.
And at the end of that long Valhalla
I pray there stood a restless paint,
saddled, stamping
and a thousand barrels waiting
out through the Milky Way.

Memento

We started with spring greens tart with vinegar.
We finished with trout baked crisp served on a platter;
our last meal together.

The morning was all May in the mountains
hemmed with green shadows of hemlock.
I took out my fly rod.

I sunk the lure in the deep V crotch of a Toe River current.
The strike ripped line from my reel
and rainbowed the rod.

Slippery muscle and fin, red-yellow spots sprayed
across brown. To shorten the tale: belly split, blood spilt,
I placed it in a pan.

Beginnings and endings blurred by brightness;
it was early summer in the South Toe Valley.
Trout were rising.

Body Electric

for Cherry

I watched you waste in one year
what took 52 to make; time-lapse rewound,
250 pound meltdown to 100
until you were no longer the electrician
that scared your union brothers.
Back magic; that was some disappearing act.

I missed your funeral
and by the time I made it back to Carolina
you were ashes on the mantle.
I walked out on the deck
where you once leaned back in a lounge chair
holding court, surrounded by your subjects
smoking dope.
Rolling numbers like you might
still get lucky in this life
shake the die, spin the wheel, make the bet—
until all of us were wrecked.

Out on that deserted deck
your absence punched me in the gut,
brought me to my knees.
I couldn't breathe, laugh, cry, shout
"Here you aren't!"
Your ghost not a presence,
but an absence,

the space where clearly you should be
but weren't.

Five of your best friends gathered later
most of us your age and counting
old enough to ignore resistance in favor of connection.
On that same deck
we fired up a fatty, toasting you;
passing it from hand to hand the way you would,
but each time we touched fingertips static snapped,
cracking as it bit.
We startled with the short sharp pain
trying it again, unbelieving—
we were grounded by the hardwood,
wore cotton clothes and sneakers.
Rubbing up against your absence were electrons
with no body to bump into
before connecting with our own.

The Gold Pocket Watch

for Marianne

This gift given from a pure place in your zen heart
a Buddhist part
with which I slowly grow familiar
is a treasure from you
so specifically for me
that I find myself a little bit afraid to own it.
This gift of a fine gold pocket watch gone
all worn and smooth, as only gold can go
came from your father's trouser pocket,
rubbed timeless by a nervous thumb,
cupped in a rough hand,
that could not tender you.
This gold pocket watch was never really yours.
After being his, stopped for all that time,
was held by you for me.
I cannot unwind the time he spent with you
always right, always on time, always telling you how it really was,
or should be,
as if you had not lived a life of full and brilliant hours all your own.

Now, my precious friend,
the pocket watch from your top drawer
which you kept because you thought you should
has found its home, its healer.
For I understand transmutation,
the snake's trick—
how to turn poison into poems,
alchemy extraordinaire.
Even as I have transformed my life
into something I could live with,

something I could maybe even love—
you remind me with your father's watch
that we cannot turn back time
and we cannot know the future.
Everything moves forward,
flows toward some gold forever,
ticks along one second at a time
with no two minutes ever just alike.
Under my thumb, I will work the magic in reverse:
turn this gold to love again
and give it back to you.

Communion

A Little Lazarus

For Leigh

> *So faith, hope, love abide, these three; but the greatest of these is love.*
> —1 CORINTHIANS 13.13

I found the tiny body lying limp on the doorstep
so small I mistook it for a bit of moving-in debris
and would have swept it away
until I caught the green glimmer of hummingbird wings.
"Look," I said, not touching it, afraid to make things worse,
not wanting even its small death on my hands.
Here is where the nursing spirit shows us common mortals up
believing as they do it's better to die loved and being loved
than all alone.
You never hesitated to lift the crumpled feathers
into the cup of your palm, whispering consolations
cooing your compassion as if you could talk it back to life.
You took it to the feeder, which you had so lovingly cleaned and filled
as I grew frustrated that you took so long at this one task
while I cleaned and mopped the entire cabin.

Like Mary and Martha, the sisters of Lazarus
on the day Jesus dropped in for a visit,
and Mary sat herself down on a stool by the Teacher
who kicked back in a recliner to share stories, swap tales,
and whisper their affections while Martha swept the floor,
fixed dinner, set the table because she knew the Lord
would appreciate it, and besides, that's what she knew to do.
And she felt left out as their laughter drifted across her sweat soaked brow,
embittering some once sweet place in her well-meaning soul
and she hollered at Mary that she "Sure could use a little help around here!"
But Mr. Intuitive, Suitor of Souls, called out to her

where she stood angrily eavesdropping there in the kitchen
"Cut it out, Martha. Mary's busy doing what Mary does best.
Now come on in here and love my neck."

And that's how it was with the hummingbird.
Like some biblical Martha Stewart I worked, worked, worked
while you performed a miracle.
Hard labor without love is just more work.
It's love that makes a miracle.
And the hummer perched upright now on your thumb
not looking the least bit frightened, only stunned.
I watched as you touched your finger to that bright and shining feeder,
drew back one glistening drop of sugar water and held it out to him.
He dipped his needlebeak and sipped it from your fingertip,
then flew. Just lifted up and flew
as if he'd never been a broken body lying on a porch step,
as if the sweetened water from a bright and shining feeder was a baptism
and you a layer-on of hands, healing
with your quiet words of comfort
and a clean birdfeeder.

I was relieved to see him go; glad that he survived
and happy too, to turn him back to Mother Nature—
into Her hands I commit his soul.
But your hummingbird heart beat after him
hoping, praying for the outcome
and I could see how your little Lazarus had chipped away
a bright green bit of God's glass from your rainbow-colored soul.

For Walt Whitman

I'm watching Whitman on a cold December morning
stride along Sixth Street.
His step snaps with purpose.
His face floats in a foggy cloud of breath and frosty beard.
He inhales the smell of roasting chestnuts,
buys a bag, stuffs them in a pocket to keep warm.
He writes as he walks;
thoughts a pen, mind a sheet of paper.
Nearing the infirmary, he sees a soldier,
doesn't care what uniform he wears.
The boy, for he is
a boy although war has aged him,
is haunted by death—
the close proximity of his own,
the ones he's witnessed,
unable to stay the cannon, musket ball or saber.
Despite the bloody bandages,
his now obvious imperfections,
the boy's eyes brighten at the sight of Walt,
papers tucked beneath his arm.

All-American poet of the people,
your gayness faded now to ghost,
something I consider queer indeed:
to make the poet less by leaving out his touch.
"My dear boy."
Whitman reaches for him,
pulls the tousled head and haunted eyes to chest.
Wooden buttons scrape the boy's big ears,

as he hears the great man's heart.
Everything about Walt quickens
tending to a youth whose rank has never called for recognition,
until now, until Whitman.
The old man cracks the chestnuts
one by one for his one-armed boy,
pops them in his mouth for him.
For the first time the blue/gray boy
feels his suffering, his sacrifices honored.
The hoary old head adores, takes him in,
can still see beauty through the shattered skin.
The poet, unafraid to touch,
strokes his greasy hair, kisses his stubbled cheek,
holds his calloused hand.
The boy feels loved.
No one has made him feel this way for years,
no matter what flag he carried, in victory or defeat.

Who are we to strip them of this moment,
forever sever poetry from the poet's nature?
Healing is what happens when we let love fill our forms:
This, poetry.
This, love.

Rules of the Road

for Malcolm Christian

Say *sawubona*.
Say *yebo, sawubona*.
When walking a dirt road in Natal
and someone passes you
who has a brown face
who is probably Zulu
say *sawubona,* which means "I see you"
or "Hello, how do you do?"
Say *yebo, sawubona* if someone should greet you
which means "I see you, too"
or "I'm fine, thank you, how are you?"

There are a thousand ways to say hello
but when our feet are tracking someone else's dust
and we're breathing someone else's air
when every bird and bush and tree is theirs to see
as they walk this road home daily
the men with hats
the women with firewood or water, washing
balanced on their heads
children in school uniforms who study you
from the corners of their eyes
say *sawubona*.
Say *yebo, sawubona*.
One word or two
coins for the toll.
It's the least we can do.

Photo Op

The Zulu woman bared her breast before the open lens
in exchange, she indicated with an empty palm,
for 2 or 4 more rand.
Leslie's eyes grew rounder than a 5 rand coin as we backed away
embarrassed by her brazenness, by what she'd do for money.
Leslie dropped the camera, looking everywhere but at her
while I couldn't help but take advantage of the moment—
my writer's eye snapped open like a window shade, a shutter,
my mind quick-photographed what I'm writing to you now:
Her breast was small, not much larger than my own
and young, (younger than I judged by studying her face)
although it drooped its head a little, the dark eye looking down.
I wondered who had fondled it or if it had fed babies yet.
I know Zulu women are not ashamed of breasts
and often in their villages they go topless, unlike Americans
or white South Africans who wear so many clothes
we couldn't flash our flesh that fast, even if we wanted.
I thought her breast quite beautiful and if I had held the camera
would have snapped the picture—
not because I cared to take advantage of the woman
(and yes I would have given her ten rand if she'd asked)
but because it was a moment rarer than a black rhinoceros,
so African, stripped free of uptight politics.
For an instant I could see the rich black soil pushed into a hillock,
waiting for the seed.
Earth and flesh as one—
how God created Eve.

Peacework

Peace by piece
patch by ragged patch
we put this quilt together.
Everybody has a story to contribute:
a tale of undeserved forgiveness
a time of unreserved generosity
some gift of grace or gratitude.
In every color of the rainbow
we stitch and sew
hoping to hold our quilt together.

Even though we'd like to forget
we know we must include
every hard-won peace,
all the patches we used to cover up the holes
we made rubbing each other the wrong way
until the whole cloth thinned
and finally gave way beneath the strain.
These, too, we must bring to the table
to negotiate our peace,
as we piece our crazy quilt together.
All that humility-toughened cotton
makes good thread
that won't come undone over time or under stress,
that can't be torn apart by malice.
We need every *I'm sorry*
I was thoughtless
Please forgive me
all the *Thank yous* we can muster
as over and over and over and under

we repeat these phrases
which serve as stitches
for the weak places in our love.
We doublestitch our mantras until we think
we've become too tired, too jaded
or that finally we've learned our lesson and can quit,
but knowing deep down the quilt is everything,
the only thing, we continue sewing peace:
red for anger
blue for hurt
green for envy
black for every hidden curse.
Next to these we put:
red for passion
blue for joy
green for healing
pink for love
black for all the magic we will need
to hold this thing together.
Peace by piece
we leave out nothing—
not the torn t-shirt from the march on Washington
or the sweat-stained blouse from the Peace Corp volunteer;
not the faded head rag worn by a civil rights grandmother
or the flowered bell-bottoms left over from the '60s;
not even the olive drabs and cammies
from the backs of our dead soldiers
or the torn corner of a flag they carried.
We use them all—
bloody rags fresh from the fists
of our perceived differences
the white sheet of surrender
the misplaced blanket of our apathy

the ticking of the cloth when we forgot
we couldn't stop
that there is always peacework left to do.
Here we are rag pickers all
until we've pieced together one story
not his story
or her story
but our story
this story
of how we put the pieces back together,
a quilt for the hope chests of our children
and our children's children.

Sunrise Service
for Jeff Davis

Why don't we all, like Indians and yogis,
naturally or ritually, *rise again* each morning
to greet the sun?
When we place our feet on the floor
with intention, with meditation, movement,
a spirit purified in clear, cold water
we can *rise again* every day;
rise up and meet the world halfway,
not wait for it to come shake us roughly by the shoulder
shouting, "You're late again!"
No, we can lift ourselves from sleep,
baptize ourselves at the bathroom sink,
step outside in robe and slippers,
stretchy yoga pants or baggy boxers,
feel the first warm rays of the sun strike our chests
and open our hearts to the fact that here we are again,
Halleluia!
Take ten deep breaths, fill the body with oxygen,
bow deeply to the light that brings us life—
our sponsor, the Sun—
then *rise again*.
Raise our arms overhead, stretch our fingers toward
invisible morning stars with childlike faith that somewhere
on yet another planet touched with magic
they, too, have a golden blossom climbing the sky like a trellis,
Halleluia!
As pastels streak the East, gray lightens to blue,
green grips the soil beneath our feet
filling with red, yellow, orange, white, lavender

flowers opening their faces to the light
and *rising, rising, rising again.*
Listen to Spring sing the song of peepers and cheepers,
promising, we all will *rise again;*
the way the memory of a loved one long gone
rolls away the stone of our forgetfulness.
Overcome by their embrace we touch their wounds,
are filled with holy communion
one being to another, no different
than a mother carries one inside the other.
The dead, they *rise again* to greet us.
See our planet say,
"Come, eat, this is my body broken for you."
Raise your crops, your children, your effigies, your prophets.
Life is not without its sacrifice.
Nothing lasts forever.
What seems gone is a simple illusion.
Rabbit in a hat.
Coin behind the ear of a child.
There's always a repeat performance.
Rise up, say "Grace."
We all *are risen*
again—
Halleluia!
Amen.

Ode to Morning

for Path's Birthday

I creep across the bare wood floors
cold heel-toe-heel
into the living room.
My buddy rises from the dead
sleep of exhaustion
peeping one-eyed
over the coffin of the couch,
grunts, "good mornin."

I've awakened due to the drop in temperature,
knowing the shitty woodstove
is only puffing smoke, nursing no blaze
so I lay a sweatshirt over her angular
frame of a strong-boned butch.
She lays back down like Dracula,
hands crossed over chest.
I find a towel to add to the pile.
Looking up I catch morning
breaking like a farm fresh egg
across the sky, yolk broken
running wet yellow streaks
fertilized with red.

Oh beautiful mountain morning
from a January cabin, be my friend's.
Be her waking up every day
give her something new to ponder, to paint.
Morning, be the hope in her heart;
stretch the day out inside her, lazy cat
waiting to be stroked, for her fur to spark;

electricity harvested from the sun
charging her creative urges
her direct connect to Life.

I have no gift but this:
May you have the morning,
bright and bleeding
heart of the world
a dozen different times of day;
cracking open
beckoning you in
to wallow in the golden glory of the Sun.

Peace in Small Packages

Sometimes peace comes in small packages:

in my neighbor's rough jokes or a sister's hug,
in my best friend's laughter at a pen pal's postcards,
in a home-cooked meal from my own vegetable garden,
in knowing the ringing phone, this time, brings hope.
Peace is in the round, flat stone my new friend found and saved for me.
It's in a loved one's lingering kiss and "You're all I need."
Peace is in my writing group circled up and scribbling,
in the knitted scarf from a friend's deft hands
that snugs my neck and keeps my teeth from chattering.
There's peace in watching children sing
and always when new writers read
their prose and poetry.

Peace is sunrise on the ocean,
sunset on the parkway,
smell of drifting woodsmoke,
crow cawing out the day.
It's stars pricking heaven,
a tree-thickened forest,
trout rising in the streams,
peace in the valley.

If the world refuses to leave peace parked in the driveway
like a rich parent's gift to a teen on Christmas day,
keys in the ignition, waiting for the easy cruise,
then let us find our peace in small packages

wrapped in everyday brown paper
parcel post delivered daily
and all too often
left unopened,
lying on our doorsteps.

Friday Nights in Yancey County

Last night we watched the full moon rise.
The fat balloon's slow ascension
backlit the winter hump of Piney Ridge.
We sat at the table finishing supper and were surprised,
as if this mellow drama didn't happen every month.
Your eyes were moonlit windows reflecting my delight
as you picked up the binoculars meant for bird watching,
not moon viewing—you need a telescope for that.
Oh, happy wrongness!
We could see the boney-fingered trees scratch
the big white belly, and between their trunks
the rhododendron hunkered, so close I thought I heard
the crackling of their leaves as they froze into cigars.
Behind it all, the moon—
huge mottled cloth of craters,
bright snow world of bluegray shadows.
Man, face, rabbit run off into space,
their memories only ghost stains on a china plate,
Rorschach ink blots where I can read our future:
Histories of Friday nights in cities with our friends
out to dinner, concerts, parties—all are past.
Our tomorrows wrap around us in the dark
holding hands, sharing these binoculars,
doing what there is to do on Friday nights in Yancey County:
Falling in love with the moon.

A Fisherman's Grace

for my brother

And passing along by the Sea of Galilee, He saw Simon and Andrew the brother of Simon casting a net in the sea, for they were fishermen. And Jesus said to them, "Follow me and I will make you fishers of men." And immediately they left their nets and followed him.

—MARK 1.16–18

From the beginning it seems
preaching the gospel and fishing have gone hand in hand,
complementary occupations, you might say—
Peter, Andrew, James, John, Dad, you;
even me, in my own way.
I keep casting for the metaphor.
Other than tall tales and swapping stories
I can't find a link until
I remember being with you in Montreat
where I watched you cast your fly in a creek not six feet wide
snagging rainbows no bigger than your hand
which you would catch and play
only to release again.
I realized then it has to do with grace
and how practicing grace has made you one
with stream and stone, overhanging tree,
the line, the fish, the fly.
You seem Grace personified,
much like Jesus was.
My clumsy casts—hook in bush,
underneath a rock, hung up in my hat—
seems I might not have that grace thing down just yet.
My line's too wild and free, lacking the control

which should connect me to the reel;
my soul, I think, more fish than fisher still.

You were so patient, kind
when you retrieved my flies, tied on different ones;
untangling my line, while you kept right on catching trout
as if the more you helped me work things out
the more the fish would come around.
I believe we could have sat down on a rock
and one by one, they would have leapt into your lap.

You never knew the greatest gift of all
was the time I spent with you; your voice
soft and low as the murmur of a stream, reminding me
how loving someone distant is one part joy and one part pain.
When you shared a hidden secret now and then,
like lures concealed inside your vest,
how my heart hung up on them
swelled and ached within my chest.

I like to think of you, half a continent away,
on Sundays in your long black robe
on Saturdays, wife and daughters at your knee
(women from our momma down are like the trout, you see).
Sometimes I think of you in the middle of the week
when I cross the road headed for the creek
and hope you're playing hooky same as me
with your waders, hand-tied flies and rod.
With luck you're trading men for fish today
and casting gracefully towards God.

The Moon's Distant Call

Last night, luxuriating
in the steaming waters of our tiny hot tub,
watching the day go down to dusk,
I saw what I thought was a hummingbird
perched in the river birch beside the steps.
She sat so still, I grew confused:
Bird . . . leaf . . . bird . . . leaf . . . bird?
She appeared to be watching the waxing moon;
slender as my little finger, green as a twig,
a furled leaf not yet flown.
I could swear she was watching the harvest moon
ballooning huge above the Ozarks.
Her tiny shoulders slightly slumped,
as if considering the long flight
from Arkansas to Mexico on one-inch wings.
But mostly she seemed, like me, lost
in the beauty of a three-quarter moonrise on a cooling breeze.
Motionless, she remained among the branches
until I gave her up for leaf at last
and looked away.
When I happened to glance back,
she was gone. Not a leaf then!
But a moon-lover like myself;
there now, sipping her last
from the feeder before bed,
as I must have my chocolate chips
to sleep through the long night
with a large moon beckoning,
keeping watch
for wherever we might land tomorrow.

Leaving

> *Consider the lilies of the field, how they grow; they neither toil nor spin; yet I tell you, even Solomon in all his glory was not arrayed like one of these.*
>
> —MATTHEW 6.28–29

On a hill above Saluda beside Pacolet Falls I lay
gazing though a screen of birch at the remnants of the day.
Not a breath, not a whisper stirred the air when,
like a camera changing focus, my stare shifted
caught the falling leaves that drifted onto clothing
slowly sifted, then gifted me, a weary warrior
with feathers for my hair.
Suddenly, I must know how each leaf fell
and how they felt about their circling descent
from heaven down to hell.
Surely after all that time so close to sky
the ground must seem an alien and far-off place to die.
No breeze shook them from their tenacious holds.
That same thin strength that held them
throughout a summer's storms seemed gone.
But wait . . . there goes one on fiery wings of gold!
Why, they're leaping from their limbs,
they're not just letting go!
They're taking turns and laughing,
they seem tickled by the sun,
as if today was a leaf parade and they're falling just for fun.
Bright red, burnt orange, soft yellow—
all dressed in Sunday finery
as they loose their perches fearlessly
for the first and last time flying

whirling, twirling, spinning 'round,
singing Hallelujahs until they gently kiss the ground.

I want to learn to leave my life as gracefully as they.
May my certain passing from this place
come to me this way—
Let me leap into forever like a well thought out adventure
leave rejoicing in the splendor of a brilliant autumn day.

ABOUT THE AUTHOR

MENDY KNOTT's diverse creativity spans poetry, memoir, playwriting, editing, songwriting, spoken-word and screenwriting. Her work reflects life as a former police officer, Air Force Veteran, and Southern "preacher's kid." In 2008 she wrote an award-winning screenplay titled "Men Only." Her first love, however, has always been poetry. Mendy's poems and performances have been featured in a long list of literary festivals, solo and benefit performances, regional publications, websites, radio programs, peace demonstrations and women's poetry anthologies. She created popular and long-running women's open-mic events in North Carolina and was honored as North Carolina Poet in Residence to South Africa in 2001. Mendy now lives in Fayetteville, Arkansas with her longtime companion, Leigh Wilkerson. Mendy also hosts *Howl: Women's Open Mic* at Nightbird Books and blogs on creativity at www.hillpoet.com.

www.ingramcontent.com/pod-product-compliance
Lightning Source LLC
Chambersburg PA
CBHW032130090426
42743CB00007B/537